THE SILK ROAD – Qing DYNASTY OF ANCIENT CHINA - The One CHINA AND TAIWAN Legal doctrine.

Diplomacy and Laws Under
PRESIDENT XI JINPING

Dr Amrit Rattan K Baidwan Macfarland

BSc(Hons), LLB, DLP, LLM, PhD, NP.

Doctor of Science, Master of Laws.

Gotham Books

30 N Gould St.
Ste. 20820, Sheridan, WY 82801
https://gothambooksinc.com/

Phone: 1 (307) 464-7800

© 2024 *Dr Amrit Rattan K Baidwan Macfarland*. All rights reserved.

No part of this book may be reproduced, stored in a retrieval system, or transmitted by any means without the written permission of the author.

Published by Gotham Books (September 14, 2024)

ISBN: 979-8-3303-5487-0 (H)
ISBN: 979-8-3303-5484-9 (P)
ISBN: 979-8-3303-5485-6 (E)

Because of the dynamic nature of the Internet, any web addresses or links contained in this book may have changed since publication and may no longer be valid.

The views expressed in this work are solely those of the author and do not necessarily reflect the views of the publisher, and the publisher hereby disclaims any responsibility for them.

WITH K MACH 10

Scientist, explorer, mountaineer, skier, aviator, Senior Airline Captain – 737, 747, 757, 767, 777, 787, 380, writer, editor, Polymath.

TABLE OF CONTENTS

PROLOGUE

The Cairngorms 1

Aphrodite and Hera.. 29

THE SILK ROAD – CHINA TAIWAN

Cairo Declaration Diplomacy 63

Cairo Declaration and Idealism As Diplomacy 66

Cairo Declaration – China and Taiwan – Dipolmatic Principles....... 68

Cairo Declaraion Diplomacy and The Rise of China 82

Cairo Declaration Diplomacy and China's Economic Ascension 83

Dipomacy Relationships of China During Its Economic and Military Rise.
.... 85

DIPLOMACY AS CAIRO DECLARATION THE TAIWAN AND CHINA ONE NATION.

Taiwan Diplomacy... 89

Cairo Declaration and The Taiwan Question..................................... 90

China's Novel Diplomacy as Belt and Road Diplomacy................... 97

China EU Europe and The Belt and Road Diplomacy 102

Summa The Cairo Declaration China and Taiwan 103

References.. 105

About The Book 108

About The Author.. 109

Napoleon Bonaparte – Dauphin of France,
with constitutional codes war and peace.

Napoleon Bonaparte, Madame Tussauds, London, Life Size

Napoleon Bonaparte in Paris Chateau de Fontainebleau, and Palace Tuileries.

PROLOGUE
THE CAIRNGORMS

"APHRODITE TO HERA – ON HIGH MOUNTAINS, PEAKS AND NATURE."

Cairngorms

Criach Ardain and Hephaestus

Criach Ardain sweet Mountain
Baking balloons
Sweet, sweet mountain
Thinking of leaving soon
Thinking of leaving soon
Will be there soon.

The colours of seasons
The words she wrote.
The hidden note
On sweet mountains
Under the stars
The glance of stars

Sweet mountain
Thinking of leaving soon
Will be there soon.
The Hephaestus grasses.
The eye of grass
The grudges of some

The world she wrote.

The hidden notes

Criach Ardain is a mountain.

Ben Hope *reaching to Poseidon.*
Poseidon and Ben Hope
High on Ben Hope
The valleys are below.
Green as far to the
Oceans of Poseidon
The heart yearning.
The wind blowing.
The days passing.
Where the years have flown

Ben Hope the wonder of me.
Time not forgotten as its memories.
The breeze is gentle here.
Cherished as one can be
Ben Hope calls
Poseidon answers the call

Ben Hope the edge of land
And cities of ices
Poised on the bank of silk
The gentle touch of a child
Here the pride is over thrown
On Ben Hope.

***Toma Choinich** and Apollo*
Toma chanting
Wandering alone far away
The hills of Toma Choinich
We all call home.

The Bothie
The rest the rain
From home
The sigh of Apollo alas
No mountain so higher

Love of Apollo
On green lands
Of snow Tome Choinich is Apollo
The whirlwind
Of waters the pale of terror
The human and the brute
No speech of prodigy
Can reach here
This is Toma Choinich Apollo's mountains.

Cairn Aosda *and Hermes*

Cairn Aosda

Hermes Scarlet

Green and blue

Sandy dunes

Cows and sheep

Eagles circling

Round and round

On the prowl

Birdies singing in the air

The cavalry of Hermes,

Equipped for dangers

Cypress hills,

Ringing bells,

Hermes says

Slack all reins

Ponies neigh

No stranger to Hermes

No stranger to Hermes

Treasure of earth

Bronze silver god

Its deeps

Hermes its fate is fulfilled

Calm Aosda

Fearless as necessity.

Ben Bheinn and Atlas
Atlas is Bhea
The sun each day
Its gives nothing away
Should I stay

I see Atlas in its shade
The sun each day
Its gives nothing away
Should I stay?

Bhea Bheinn is in the way,
Its sun getting
Larger each day
Its gives nothing away

Oh give us more
Atlas Bea Bheinn
The foothold the sun
Each day
Its gives nothing away
Shall I stay?
Atlas is on my gates
The sun shines everyday
It gives nothing away
Should I stay?

Yes Atlas is Bea Bhenin

The signpost on the door
The sun shines everyday it gives nothing
Away
Should I stay
Through valleys and ridges
Row upon row
Granite as dark
The sun shines
Every day
Its gives nothing away shall I stay
Ben Bhenin
Bea Bhenin
Atlas Atlas
Its laurel boughs
Bhea Bhenin
Bhea Bhenin.

Ben Vane *the fiery mountain and Dionysus*

Ben Vane and Dionysus
The fire in the mountain
Long distance runner
Dragon and fires
Ablaze as fire and ice,
Merciful and fiery
Passionate and dashing
Ben Vane
Long distance runner
Holding out the flame
Ben Vane
Ben Vane
Ben Vane
Fire ice Dionysus.
And Mountain
This god various and subtle
Who is pursuant?
As unalienable
Is Ben Vane
Ben Vane
Ben Vane.

The song of Mountains **Braeriach Ben**
The songs of the mountains
Braeriarch, I hear her calling
This song as sounds of the mountains.
Through the woods
End to end Phrygian.
As sheep pastures
These Pamphylan hills
The sound of Ben, as words
Of the past,
The sun rises, the sun goes down.
Through the words to the
Music of the mountains
We ran.
The whirling wind, this
Endless power,
This tender strength
The breath of godhead.

The sound of music the sun rises
The sun sets
La la whoa la la
We sleep the sun goes up
The sunrise the sound of music,

Cairn Eije *sound and thunder of Helios*
Helios Helios
Nectar of the gods
Cairn Eige a
Ruchus makes
Clear streams blue
Eyes, come to see
Look Helios on the mountain
The drums they beat the way
The heart, the art
The matter, the key is Helios
The angel of Cairn Eige the same
The sound of drums, the whistler
Of the road,
The chance taken,
With Helios the supreme
The favour of an ancient race,
Helios cair Eige
Its watchful eye
Is Cairn Eige.

Ben Lomond

Ben Lomond
Athena the voice of Ben Lomond
Sharp strides, strong feeling
The climb
Direction, and movement
Fairy taking
Knocking down,
Breaking speaking
Silence pushing
The climb
The side is Athena
As colour
Impatience
Worlds flames,
As leaping devouring
The joy of kindness,
The heeded stock of Athena
Is Ben Lomond.

Ben Anon *and Artemis*

Ben Ben Ben Avon
Atremis proud and tall no canyons
No earth to ear
The wind and stream
As flow

Ben Ben Ben Avon
Artemis proud and tall this company
The proud Anon
The wind and stream as flow
Artemis rolling and rain leaf in the
Air, ear to ear,
Ben Lomond

Ben Artemis
The roaming
The landing
The flight
The scrambling
Ear to ear
Ben Lomond

Ben Lomond Ben
Lomond time is
Clinging to the peak
Is here
Cool rivers

Artemis Ben Lomond
Ben Lomond

My home is Ben Lomond
Ben Lomond is
Artemis.

Blue edge mountains **Benin Ime**
The blue mountains of Benin Ime
Ime, Ime, let us lie down
Here, this stormy shine
The welcome of green
Eyelids the careless
Flutter of wings, a snake
In the hedge,
A wooden nest,
Ares as loveliness
A sea to avoid
Toiling hard
Coming the orchard gate
Heart melting glances
Of Ares, this god of Benin Ime,
As Erasmus
The gentle water
Rich moisture
Benin Ime,
Benin Ime,
The benevolent.

***Ben Lawers** wee Mountain of Artemis*
Ben Lawers is all you need
As first step it is a
Small mountain
Its feet of Artemis
Fortune bringer
Good well
Day counted
Mulled wine
No weeds on show
Only snow
The snow and dance of
Of foxes galore
Then Artemis as piety
Runs down the small mountain

Good fortune
Why prove me wrong
Speaking if you wish
Attending carefully
This wee and small
Mountain as one
Ben Lawers, is
You call to your mission and dreary Cairngorms.

Dreary Cairngorm

The mythical mountains
Of Apollo
One morning as the sun rose and the
Pines were ablaze
With the sun,
The track was winding
We were heading this way
The crystal streams
The bird so colourful
And bright the birds all honoured
Him
As Derry Cairngorms
This big mountain the full trees
And corns
The barns full of hay,
The trickling fountains
And wolves and foxes awes and picks
Were laid
When Apollo came in
On Derry cairngorm
The masters and cousins
The whole crew
Fixed on the immovable.

Sgurr Nan Gillean

The mountains meet pulls map
Sunny clouds no dim days
Bright tomorrow when I close
My eyes I see
Sgurr Nan Gillean

Through ice and fire as volcanic
Co creators
Unstoppable as force of nature
The hymns
Of Sgurr Nan Gillean

The deer rise up to the peak
The valleys full of blue purpose
Heather this is the majesty of
Sgurr Nan Gillean

She is the fighter as born
And me, passing the test,
Merits and flame,
The dream is born next,
The snow
Blizzards thunder
Rain winds rivers
Tides, the hymn of
Sgurr Nan Gillean.
Sgurr Nan Gillean

Betrays nothing
No secret no thought
The surrender to
Sgurr Nan Gillean
This caress of snow
As gardens formative
Of only Sgurr Nan Gillean.

Ben Starav -mountains at my doorstep
Ben Starav, Ben Starav,
The mountain at my doorstep
More each day, it gives
More takes and stays

Ben Starav this mountain at my doorstep
A fire unites a lake
It is a rolling mountain
With no brakes
Looming larger, every day.

Ben starov, Ben starov, a singing
Out signalling
Each day,
Fire in its lake flame
In its heart
Standing your ground is Ben Starov,

It is the lungs, the voice
The choice is Ben starov
The mountain at my doorstep.

Cairngorms **Bendaloo**
Yeah, Yeah I breathe you
The Cairngorm
Precious darling I love you
I see you, I want to know you
No slippery slope
But solid ground
One in five million
I kiss its grounds
Hey Hey I love you

What have we to lose, the
Bendaloo, moves
I move,
It sees, It does I do
Bendaloo Bendaloo we sing.

So what did we lose nothing said
Bendaloo, now I have come home,
Sing sing loud
And clear
Cairngorms
Bendaloo we are coming
We are coming
We are coming
Do you hear us,
And Yes, I have come home.

Blue Ridge Mountains and fleet of foxes
Cairnwell, Cairnwell, De Cairns of the well,
My dear Cairns the night stormy
This secret what should we do tonight,
I missed my connection, the connecting
Flight, go climb a mountain,
Cairnwell, as welcome sight,
Any time you like,
The countryside is wild
And roaring, shiny do not get reckless.
Be bold but not reckless
The quivering pines,
The red foxes, the golden eagle,
Ushering the way,
A nest of falcons,
The rivers frozen,
Let us not get snowed in
The moon is yellow and Andromeda breaks in
Cairnwell sees Andromeda
Entering the milky way
Shivering shuddering the sky ablaze,
The gold of the falcon
Frantically circling
The winged driver
The gardens of Zeus
Nourished only by melting snows,
The river frozen,
Cairnwell

Cairnwell

The pangs of Andromeda

Looming a child

Without any fault

These Teuthras sheep pastures

Go climb a mountain

Cairns, Cairns, Cairnwell.

Summit Climb

Suilven the summit

See, it, dreamer,
Dreaming doing beauty
The climb,
The reach,
The steps, the feelings
The one direction,
The climb to the summit of summits

No struggle the snow
As falling, the deer is charming
Assisting not taking down
The moments of suilven,

Remember keep remembering
No ordinary mountain
Suilven,
Morning losing
The other side,
Morning glaciers,
Climbing keep climbing the summit
As Suilven.

Cairn Toul

A moving mountain

Moving mountains

The rock the hurricane

The promise

Obliterate the malevolent

Quarantine the dragons travelling

The high and through the mountains

The agony thirst

Aside the fifth man at the Borrean gate

The threshing floor of a shield

The moving mountain

Moving the mountains

The water fall,

The shielding stone

The Neistan gate

The restless mares

The charged mares

The toss the turn

The proud heart beats

The breath of music

Trembling at the gates of Cairn Cairn

Cairn Toul

The moving mountain.

Ben Lui

The misty mountain
And snow cold
Gold peaks, mighty bells, ancient kings
Gleaming sword
Shapes and shadows
Gems and rain

The dwarfing lands
Silver parks
Flowers and stars
The blinding moon
And sun

Rain Rain, the break of day,
The not forgotten
Land a perpetual
Cause
The green pines
Roaring at heights

The Ben Lui song
The fires red, blazing, torch,
Fierce and frank the feet of some
Grim notes,
The harps and songs the mist descending
the single dwelling
one mind

one heart
as firm resolve
the force of sight
melting as rule
love and Joy
honour and character of Ben Lui.

Binnein Moir

Binnein Moir, the fire of the moon
Thunder alleys sun shining
The flute and trombone, the keys
The kitchen down time
Looking good and clear,
The soul expanding
The heart understanding
Rolling thunder drums
Sleeping music
Rising grounding
Servants popping
Speed the perfect glories and
North winds.

Picking speed, the wonder of the sweet day,
Standing beside
The king,
Raising hands,
A thousand sun shines.

The scrambling for first place
The beating heart, and drums
Confessions made
The love of God
Companion all of you
As strong towers

No mean scale
No duet and best
But scrolls as mountains
No fallen men,
This soul of confidence
The orchestra, the champion.

APHRODITE AND HERA

Immortals of Time

Aphrodite and Hera saw the immortals of time,

they were there at the same

Time, and how the ten, gods and their armies and swords,

as not one two three, four, five, six, seven, eight, nine, ten,

down four and a half centuries, they kept on and on coming, nothing could stop their coming once the event began.

Handsome, fiercely shining, with beautiful emblems, for 450 years they cascaded down from the mountains of Kashmir like rolling hills.

He first took his stand against the then evil emperor, corrupt and most vile, Taking him down, ruinous and evil was his ending.

The Arcadians understood and recorded the same as did the Greeks who knew Kashmir through Alexander the Great, who had been married of the same but the second was the same, the flood of deedless acts did flow watering weeds a loathsome flow of men, as emperors the same, monsters of time, the Sphinx of the grand mountains she bore as witness this bearer of time and history, the ramparts rammed hammered, by the second and so it became, each emperor had a God standing directly opposing, his every move and stance, in opposition then to his Heart's core, as vengeance, their hair stiffened, in terrors most awesome, as gods be gods, we all know, they were gods, invincible not human at all, the immortal horde, destroying men in battle, the men fought bravely, under their emperors, but strong Amphiaraus was not stationed, at the Harrobean gate, as before, they the gods undid all they had taught, the citizens of their evil ways, Avengers as gods, from above, their gaze upturned, seekers of strife not peace, to remove the ten ominous names, obliterating the malevolent, and quarantining the dangerous once and for all time and eternity, no one to assist the cause for they came out of nowhere, and the rage of the heavens, accompanied them all and one by one down the centuries never ceasing once the event had begun, the pious god men, across the bay, from the impious men emperors of time, the fate of these sealed by these gods, they much abhorred and hated.

Aphrodite and Hera -the King of Thebes

Aphrodite, Aphrodite, and Hera,
Aphrodite, Aphrodite, Hera, Hera,
Hera, Hera, Aphrodite, Aphrodite,
Hera, Hera, Aphrodite, Aphrodite,
Aphrodite against the Ten,
Aphrodite and Hera as One,
The sisters of Etocles,
The King of Thebes,
Antigone Ismene, no match,
For Aphrodite,
As the daughter of Venus,
The champion of Thebes, an Aryan born,
From above,
Born and bred,
She is the beauty of our time,
Aphrodite and Hera as one,
She who holds the helm
She who bridges Pilots
She works through sleepless nights,
She the country's greatest good fortune,
She who speaks when the Hour demands,
She who gives her due to Venus,
And the heavens of her own galactic sun
Solus as supreme is Aphrodite
She when heaven, forbids falls silent,
She when ills confront
Calls on Etocles, the harped wings,

When threats and wailings siege the lands,
She the protector of the lands,
Your part now Hera says,
The staunch young man,
To greatness then as duty calls
The honour of our gods, never tarnished,
Guarding our children, grandchildren, their children,
She who weighs the scales of Justice,
She who weighs the scales of fortunes,
She who gives us the best of peace,
She who with the help of the Alamos fires,
Reflects as most noble,
Returning, again and again in another guise,
Time and again,
Shone the eyes, as fixed as an army,

Adrastus and the chariots of fire,
She beckons,
Takes him home to her parents,
Hearts as iron blazed,
The light of a lioness,
The Ship's captain, the thunder of hoofs,
Changes time swiftly,
The Judges are let loose,
The sound I grows nearer,
As Time switches, it gears to tenth,
This goddess of time
The pleadings through robes and wigs on display,

The golden helmet of grace,
They guard us our country,
Seething the seven ugly sisters, of disgrace,
The breath of Ares drives
To another place and time
These the agonies of time
Encircling the fortress of Hera
Again and again,
This pure virgin daughter
Of grace, Venus, Leo, Apollo,
As the gods ordain,
A marriage of the same,
Taking their vows afresh, and their
Renewed time in History,
Dear son of Odysseus, why the objections
Have been overruled, calm and quiet,
Walk and talk the gods
Who share our life and destiny,
Never forsaking those green walls,
No curses may enter,
Only true and blue friends,
The garlands of Aphrodite,
As certain as the Sun,
A kind soul of Ares,
At our gates of Tydeus,
Stands and roars
Not forbidden but
Invited in by this time,

The skilled most pre-eminent
Fail as falling
As tarnished stars of time,
The eyes of night thunder
In the Venus, Jupiter, as their full
Glorious full beam,
Madly exultant these our river banks
The trustworthy, no scorn,
The chafing trumpet blasts,
Blows them clear away,
The gates of Proteus opens
And the barrier falls,
Speech, fiery courage,
Strength our protection,
The grace of Hera, not Artemis,
This our Champion and our god!

Aphrodite to Hera Hey I had a dream!!

Aphrodite to Hera,
Hey I had a dream,
Aphrodite tell me about it,
Actually I had a run of dreams,
Hey tell me about it,
At first I could not make the meaning of them,
But as they continued to flow like rivers of the mountains,
It all began to make sense,
Hey tell me about it,
Yes, in the dream it began with my usual run of the day
I was running the same place, the same time,
The same route, next to the river over the bridge, and back,
Then what happened,
It was not like an ordinary run,
The run began quickened like I was flying
With the touch and breath of Zeus himself,
Were you,
Yes, I was then what
I came to the bridge and I was standing on it alarmed,
The river had swollen to such an extent, it had risen right up to the
Bridge,
I stopped and stared at the waters they were
Overwhelming,
The swans had risen, with the waters, and were swimming like crazy,
The waters were not gleaming waters,
What were they
They were a dull grey

Like the skies,
They were grey waters,
Then I looked across the bridge,
It had broken in half,
And half of the bridge, had been consumed, by the waters,
Then what
In the dream, I began analysing what I saw
I realised I was very lucky
I was on the safe side, of the bridge,
At the right time in the right place,
Seconds later I could have been
In the wrong place and in the wrong time,
The chambers of the earth had saved me,
From getting trapped and falling,
But these waters had overwhelmed
Many others and their sun had set
Then I met a friend the same one
She gave me some thing
A falcon flew overhead, with a guide at the helm as upright,
It gave me a silver thing then said do not be alarmed,
All is well do not despair,
Then the same friend, came again,
And showed me a book it was a PhD
Then she showed me another book
It was a book of poems, then she hugged me,
And told me I am fine,
Then she took her phone and told me
Richard is fine,

Richard you can trust him,
Then I was swimming and met Richard twice,
I was back at the bridge, and the waters had subsided,
And they had become very dark and ditchy,
The bridge was rebuilt and was in tact,
And the waters were no longer water but Oil,
Dark, murky, and dirty,
Together with my friend we ran
Back to the house,
And this time there was an open sea, in front of us,
And a bridge,
And we began stacking our books and placing
Them in boxes ready to depart, to some place else,

Aphrodite and Hera one and the same
Aphrodite not Athena Hera not Athena
Aphrodite and Hera not one and the same
Athena God willing will sack this town and not
Wait for the counterblasts of the Zeus the same
Stop, stop the lightning's and thunderbolts, now Zeus
Athena said it is only midday
What is in your head?
Is it a weapon or a blazing torch
Or is it golden letters from above
Or is it to challenge a hero
Or it is to grow from gain to gain
Or is it still to be proud as Miss folly
Or is to so your tongue is unbridled, and loose and free
Or is it like Copernicus not mere words, only a defiance,
Or is it crazy exultation
Or full lungs saved as full strengths
Or is it some mortal challenge
Unbecoming to the heavens
Or is it swelling waves of unrest
In your tender breast
Or is it guiding speech
Much like Aphrodite, and Hera?
Or is it fury without courage
Or is it loud boasting or bursts of insolence,
As free speech, to spear and hurt the innocent,
Or is it to make a maiden so fair retreat into desolation,
What is it?

Or is it you want to leap and crow
Or is it restless mares in nightmares
Or ladders into enemy walls
Or is it to disgrace the race and sons of Creon,
Or is it boasting where no boast remains
Or is it to brag about champions, as defendants of your home,
Or is it to avenge the Athena or Happomedon,
That tall handsome splendid figure you so love to hate
What is it?
Or is it Typhon in your mouth
Like black smoke
Rotting your guttering or
Is it hollow and fat belly
Drunk on lusts and Pallas
Or Oenops as Hermes
As knocks now on your doors.

Aphrodite and Hera
Noted

Aphrodite and Hera

Noted when man's pride spills into folly

What hope is there

Cast at his feet not like Zeus

Lightnings and thunderbolts

My Oh My said Aphrodite to Hera

My Oh dearie me, said Hera to Aphrodite

Such fire bearers these earth men

In the midheat of humanity

The golden letters not of Venus

Not mercury

The challenges reached us

In the heavens

A giant like bloater was seen

In outer space,

Was it a balloon

No said Aphrodite

It is made in China I think

Surely not

It must be a balloon

Or a bird

Or worse still space debris

Hera and Aphrodite

The Venusian most intellect norm,

Making her

Moving her

To her grandest form,

Level I man

Level II man

Level III cosmic man

The grandest human cosmic norm,

Aphrodite as Venus, not as Earth, knows her and has made her

But the original form, as Aphrodite, the most superior of a female Norm,

She came when Venus was once earth,

Three earths as one, Venus, Mercury, Earth,

The superior self as cosmic no longer human,

The speeches of the human prodigy,

Zeus and Aphrodite, as one and the same thing,

Cosmic and galactic frames,

Moving their solar antennae, to gather

Intellect and poetry as substance and norm.

Aphrodite to Hera What?

Aphrodite you passed,
Hera what?
Aphrodite you passed the litmus test, life presented you,
You passed with flying colours,
Hera me personally,
Aphrodite yes, you personally and those you love,
Hera me,
Aphrodite yes on an individual level
Therefore you redeemed everyone you love,
I am Greek and gave philosophies to the world,
On how to think, straight, in clear lines, by formulating
First the correct thesis,
Hera yes,
Now we have all ascended the ladder with you my dearest
Aphrodite,
Yes, Hera?!

Aphrodite and Hera

Loved much
They loved their men far too much
For all our men are gone forth
Said Aphrodite to Hera,
Echo, Sierra, Oscar,
Sierra, Sierra, Oscar,
Oscar, Oscar, Oscars,
But of a different kind
As urgent emergency calls,
Two thoughts the same,
Two girlies the same,
Aphrodite and Hera,
Hera and Aphrodite
Pressed the stop button at once,
Their own names.

Aphrodite and Hera

Troubles came, like a sea of rolling waves,
They solved them together, as problem solvers, the same,
Aphrodite and Hera,
The surges,
The seething waves,
The barrier between life and death,
They manipulated all this together,
As two space scientists
Measure the width of the wall,
The line of kings,
Made the settlement not heavy,
The vast wealth of times,
In the hands of a few
Fall Persians prostrate at our feet,
But the Persians and Greeks knew better
These two old and trusted friends.
When Aphrodite sang her Venus songs,
To be honoured and not forgotten, her friend,
Her best friend, no her bestest friend, Hera,
Heard her, and joined with souls to form her
Advocacy, as soft persuasion,
It did not come from earth,
Earth humans were too coarse and grounded,
In the mud of the physical,
When Hera, she made the music
Aphrodite, wrote the books and poems,
Then they assigned it to the Ben mountains, for editing, which

He duly did,
The purpose of Aphrodite,
As Venus on earth, was to be stronger,
Force and frontier,
Never out of step,
Her marriage to solus,
Made her climb, even higher on his high shoulders,
And they had the protection of the seraphic limbus,
At the solar ray, that enclosed both of them,
Nowadays they call it angel, but it is a solar form,
The mind of Aphrodite, was unfathomable, but she
Was uncompromising,
About her stay her time on earth,
And Solus he kept her free from all afflictions,
This her reward for being Aphrodite.

Aphrodite to Hera,
So what has Paris in common with Rome,

A lot

They are one and the same thing

Not diametrically opposed,

The line of rising humanity

The rage of angels

Through time

The intellect of angels,

Their names as spoken,

A toast to our New King!

Aphrodite to Hera

Let us go to the land of the immortals,

But I have already been,

Yes, I was born there,

Still let us go again,

You can show me the places, in town?

Whatever do you mean?

Well, just as I said, he is not at once,

Explain, I will first let me see Megareus,

If he is awake, to take down notes,

This sown race of the immortals,

Lived high up in the mountains,

Up as boasting of him,

No wild din of snorting horses,

That drove them trembling from the valleys

And the gates,

Only leopards as snow are their type and kinship

This is their native soil

As the first human Aryans as

Their spoils of grace,

Like champion brags,

Leaving nothing out

Only the best mountaineers, and skies

See them.

Waving, laughing, speaking beautifully

Them to their success now and then cheering

The gods they are of the lens of the mounds,

Of centuries upon centuries of the

Aryan civilization but first
They were the immortals.
 Aphrodite to Hera
Abortive missions there but rescue missions here,
Yes, Yes, my friend is the best soul on earth,
Kennedy Yes, I know that
Berlin, yes I know that
Cuba, Yes, I know that
Arabia is here now,
Yes I lived it, and the fire and much worse,
Like hell of genocide on planet earth
The prospects of the future in the hands of immortal Cashmere,
Something no one tells you on the battlefields,
Run as fast as you can with feet like chariot wheels,
The King himself came knocking on my door,
Are you well are you well, we love you so dear,
Could not bear to lose you now, not ever,
Just in time, to hear the messengers news
The quickened stride the sense of urgency over us all
The acute and grave time of history, for the bravest of all the lands,
The order of the defence of the realm,
Yes, Yes, I know exactly the disposition of an extremely noble friend,
I can tell you who posted the gate,
I can tell you Tydeus failed on the stand with roars,
I can tell you the cross of Ismenus is forbidden here,
I can tell you this was not favourable,
I can tell you the son of Oecles skilled as he may be is scrap
I can tell you the helmet's mane was worn by One.

Aphrodite to Hera, is there life in the Universe,

Of course there is because
You and then I are the Universe
We are gods remember, do not forget,
Yes of course, of course Aphrodite, and Me Hera, as one,
See how we return again and again
See how we are indestructible,
See how we cannot be killed as we are invincible
See how the frenzies get uttered again and again
See the venom and hatred in them,
See how the families are strangers, and strangers,
As star crossed voyagers become lovers,
See how Chalybes came with Scythia from one and the same place,
See now steel is cast and assigned
See how the dead men think they are Great,
See how the spreading plains have no share,
See how the earth brings us close as one,
See how the crimson blood blackens and never dries,
See them with their agonies,
See how old vintage is mixed with new,
See how swift the judgements come
See the third generation as Laius and Apollo
See how Pythian is rising from the earth's navel,
See how the oracles are speaking
See how love returns
See how inheritance is apportioned,
See how the last words of man are forgotten as God,
Echo, echo, Sierra, Sierra, Oscar, Oscar, are coming

See how a mother's dying wish is abandoned,
See how Erinys returns with courage,
See Apollo was the dread as Commander of the sevens,
See is there life in the universe,
Yes, it is there and now it is here.

Hera to Aphrodite, What a journey

What a journey
The King and I
The Queen to her awesome King
Your Majesty supreme and glorious
Of tens of thousands, of rolling years,
Unknown by some
But I know that you are the Majesty of Space and time,
Given to us from on high,
Your Queen awesome and beautiful
Her glorious curls her stare fixed on only one goal
My precious darling
On You, on you, on you,
Look what a journey she has made,
Such beauty, such glory, such a pain and ordeal
Bestowed on the best in the world,
The Heavens will never fail you, nor they you,
Take care of her a second chance given,
For you are a king of the line of Kings,
Of billions of glorious years know this first
May he grant you joy, love, peace, and abundance,
As you deserve a great rest and glory after this,
Your healing hands did this,
Your prayers were heard by the Himalayas, ,
They their witness as one,
You know her,
The will of heaven rules,
It rules us always has done,

For we are the champions, skiers, mountaineers,

Of the Himalayas and Cairngorms,

Having traversed 48 Everest and ben Macdui in a lifetime

What a prayer to the cosmos,

They have come to you my sweetest dearest friend,

Most cherished of time,

The messengers come with chariot wheels,

Unknown by all

They come with speed,

They quicken their speed and urgency,

For all is restored in time,

By champions, the same as you,

The plunderer loaded and gone.

The royal place, of Xeres in the Kanchenjunga,

Your royal mother, she knows it all

The fearless pharandaces came again and again,

So a golden knight of our time, Sosthenes, came to

Sikander which is You,

Your grandmother knows she saw you before

You arrived, one so great and noble,

A Knight of Sagittarius

Your father a Sagittarius,

The great King Ariomardus, is us

The great river of time,

My sweetest and the greatest of all

Time,

Your deeds are noted by another place in time

The place from which you came to us

Kissane ramparts are you with their
Ten million legions on earth now arrived
From Jupiter to secure your gates,
Sent by Heaven only for you,
My most precious darling,
Enjoy sit back and never forget the skies,
They are you.

Aphrodite to Hera, so what else

What else you must be joking, what else,
What else, what else,
This is a unique type of alpha and Omega,
The cold war as history,
Yes so, so what are you on about?
The enlargement of Moscow as a reflection of Russia's historic
Experience,
So what has this got to do with the Gods of the Mountains,
A Lot bear with me,
Aphrodite but that is old history ancient even
Did your best friend teach you all this
Well yes, he is from the mountains, he knows all
Things as he is quantum man,
Not just physical and he is of the order of the defence of
The grand mountains, he flies over them,
Oh I see, where is all this leading to I am lost
You lost with your clarity of thinking
Yes said Aphrodite amused I know
About the tragedy of Poland which year
1935 -1945 said Hera Next?
The fall of Romania, Hungarian, Bulgaria, and Czechoslovakia?
Yes them too
So then what happened, this is not gossip this is fact
Aphrodite to Hera, Yes I am all ears do go on,
I am Venus and you are Mercury,
As I was saying the American behaviour is reflection of the Russian
Experience and vice versa,

Yes so then the creation in 1945, the power vacuums on either,

Yes Still Russia's conquest of the Baltic states and east Poland was the trigger in 1939-1944

Stalin all are Mountain men.

Aphrodite to Hera the unchanging oceans,

The Unchanging Oceans,

Oceans the country of laurel boughs

Oceans deep and silent seas
Oceans a duty written on our palms, and hands

Of Oceans as third

Think of me Oceans of Time,

Keep remembering the promises

Oceans of Apollo, in our youth in this time

Think of me as two hearts beating in

Two different worlds,

Oceans the same now and then,

Oceans its crops and fruits

As unchanging as the seas

Think of all the things we said

And did, think of all the things

We shared and saw

Think of all the things without you and me,

Think of all the things always

The same as Oceans and seas,

The Oceans our country,

Free and wild

Silent and tempestuous

Our silent reverence to Zeus

As coming home,

The gods the oceans as university

Never changing

Reflected in us

You and me.

Think of Aphrodite,

Her garlands of snow

Think of her power

The Argive, Artemis

The sword of Ares,

Zeus of the Oceans, is

In you and in me

Oceans as laws of justice

As duty written for the fourth

That is you and me,

Think of us when waking

Silen or resigned

For you are me

And I am you, since

Immortal of times,

Oceans and Seas,

Flowers fade and summers

Come and go

But oceans are us are free

And never fade

The ships are sailing

As You and Me

The oceans reflected in us

As Aphrodite and Artemis

Or Zeus and Aphrodite or even Argive.

Hera My sun of suns my galaxy

The fleet that take time as putting out

To oceans and sea, time coming of our Galaxy

No captain, no anchor dropped

No ship as shepherding

No harbourless coast,

No sundown no fall of night

A good steersman no force or thrust

Proper landing as craft

Here comes our galaxy as Sun of the suns

His seat the clear blue air,

From drifting clouds to snow

The smooth summit reached

No dizzy crags

No vulture haunted

No plunges into the abyss

These the citizens of our Galaxy.

Aphrodite and He came

He came the road to hell is paved with good intentions,

He came,

He came,

He came

A fiery forge

A gentle stream

A firm cosmic handshake

A firm furnace ignited

The French statute of liberty

The winners the long before this

At the UN Senate

Votes 400

Comes with winners

He came,

He Came,

And He came,

As the central sun with twelve planets around him

He came.

Hera Living up to your name

Living up to your name

The magical aspects is the name

The voice of the name as

Fluid, personal, emotional,

It intimates personal presence, behind

The text, speaking as directly to us

Is living up to your name, as your name,

And only your name as given

A name is talismanic

There is more in your name

Than you can ever imagine

It is your manifest destiny as one

It deletes the imagery of caged birds

The glimpsed sheen of the eye of your

Name is talismanic

Charges the loves the word play it is

Your delicious suggestions

To the world and a sense of another proximate

World its vibration resonates,

Through this world as your manifest

The name is the active galactic nucleus

With which you are born and from moment to moment

Second to second, and through eternal time

It is a super massive solar system,

The centre than attracting the same

Galaxies that come running

And spinning as discs

This other worldly nature
Is your name your name
As given, it is your manifest destiny as
Universe on earth,
And the silent self doting cosmos within
Is your name as given
Living up to your name as given.

Aphrodite Akash Ka Farishta

Akash Ka Farishta is the name of the first angel on earth
This Akash Ka Farishta is my twin
The personification of the other world
From the wide open spaces of 45,000 glaciers
The heavens above of Sagarmatha
The glory of these mountains
Forgotten by mortal man
The earth its mountain fires
The rivers coming from them,
This figure of eyes that laugh
And do not burn,
Is the Akash Ka Farishta of the glory mountains
Mountain we are coming Mountain we are coming
Please help us to ascend to thine peaks
47.5 times in a lifetime only.

THE SILK ROAD
—
CHINA TAIWAN

CAIRO DECLARATION DIPLOMACY

The Cairo declaration was concluded at the Cairo Conference in Cairo Egypt on 27th November 1943, those attending were President Franklin Roosevelt, of the United States, Prime Minister Churchill of the United Kingdom, and Generalissimo Chiang Kaishek of the Republic of China. The science of international laws as Roman jurisprudence came into play, this science of legislation, comprises the ability on the part of international law making by Nations bilaterally or multilaterally are the measures taken to minimize pain and misery, post world wars, and to restore nations to their best positions, prior to wars. The art of the legislation is the ability of Nations, as Heads of state, to make treaties which would post world wars, create laws under sound roman law maxims, scientific universal immutable principles of Higher laws, those that would effectively promote the good of nations that have suffered wrongs, post world wars, and reduce the high impact of the deleterious devastating, damaging actions as bad in this sense.

The roman felicia calculus ensures this through its equation, as and through diplomatic means to use power, friendship, national pride and good reputation, benevolence, to reduce via the norms of many and multiple scientific principles as laws, privation, fear, enmity, bad reputation, malevolence, and using the felicific calculus of using the factors of good intentions, noble intent, and measure through these with purity of actions, the damage caused its duration, its intensity, its certainty, its fecundity, propinquity, through wars conducted on them, illegal migrations and usurpation of their lands by illegal means by enemy nations, and reduce all wrongs done in this sense.

The Cairo Declaration of one China and One Taiwan was ratified on the 1st of December 1943. All Chinese islands in addition were to be restored to the Republic of China and Japanese illegal migrants were asked to leave all territories including Taiwan; taken under the norms of wars. This quantitative measure chooses to perpetrate good over the bad done, and then to enact laws, which would have the balance and overall effect of restoration to prior position before wars were waged on them. Clause 8 of the Potsdam declaration further endorsed the One

China Taiwan (islands) principle and in addition to Taiwan also Penghu became as one as part of the Republic of China. The ROC further clarified the ratification of a further numbered article - the declaration of China Taiwan, under Ma Yu Geon, that this was deemed under international laws, a legally binding instrument. Later treaties, and documents were endorsed, ratified, reaffirmed, and rendered by all of these as standing and of time, that the Cairo Declaration was legally binding.

Since Cairo Declaration, Taiwan has become a controversy, the declaratory was ratified post world wars that Taiwan is the territory of China, several developments, and theories that have arisen with relation to both China and Taiwan. Academics have tried to interpret the one China system, based on the characteristics of both China as a rising power, and many fear that it would behave the same way as USA to dominate the regions of the world, to augment its national interests and security. The Rise of China, is the new thesis and it focuses on its relationship to its military, economic base. Taiwan as one China policy and its belt and road initiative is China's Taiwan policy as endorsed by the legitimacy of the Cairo Declaration, remains unchanged, much to the chagrin of the western nation states, especially the USA.

The rise of China sits in the balance of power axis US and allies and Russia and its allies as BRICS nations. Diplomacy foreign affairs, is the instrument through which a China and Taiwan can be examined with accuracy.

China along with BRICS challenges US and allies as a power in Asia major and minor and the world. US often accuses China as undemocratic and violating human rights and often not following the norms of the classic roman jurisprudence as Rome statutes, that dictate to international laws, and China has reverse onused USA the same as through the lens of the war on terrors in Afghanistan, and the Middle east for over two decades. USA has levied fresh charges that China intervenes in its market and ignores all rights by doing so.

Chinese democracy is not the same model as the west as it is an ancient jurisprudence and polity. The balance of power pushes on US allies and Russia and allies as one against the other. International politics have an anarchical political structure since the last two decades, due to the terms

USA has been using, the notion of maximisation of its national security. The actors of both sides, have military power at their disposal to further destruction, and then nations survival becomes the central norm, fear and irrationality dominate power cultures, and the strongest state feels the safest, Nazi Germany, USA, Soviet Union, were the powers of the past, and tried to dominate other countries. China may mimic the same model it is conceived by scholars. The balance of power, has been shifting towards China. China's belt and road initiative promises hope for nations, as China's weight in the balance of power, is increasing. China states its foreign policy is peaceful, the strategic importance of Taiwan, remain to China as law deems it and the laws and treaties post world wars are still active and in force.

CAIRO DECLARATION AND IDEALISM AS DIPLOMACY

There are many themes as classical in diplomacy and idealism is superimposed on real events, and has a special place in diplomatic literature, since ancient times, the first treatise, the Aryan Indus civilization, the art, and sciences of diplomacy was conceived as the Artha shastra. The globalisation of world politics is nothing new, and makes for a complicated realism. Idealism has always been the true dominant theory of diplomacy and Just legal principles underlying them as foundational, this theory its applications, have always been sound to keep the world stable and functioning at full efficiency. The tradition is understood through principles application of roman Ius gentium and is essential for understanding how Diplomacy must work as an instrument through international politics and helps a better understanding of the international relations theories and politics. All diplomatic theories are aligned with the idealism realism paradigm. These theories are as old as time itself, and their formulations, evolve over time with different cases and situations.

The origins of idealism go back to the Artha Shastra as first diplomatic treatise, followed and adapted by others such as Thucydides, and written on by philosophers such as Machiavelli, Hobbes and other well-known scientists and the diplomatic mechanisms, now exist post world wars I and II, to settle wars as quickly as possible.

In the twenty years, middle east crisis, there has been a shift away from idealism ignoring the importance of scientific principles and substituting it with power as the only tool at the heart of politics. A minor theory never applauded was used by Politicians in the war on terrors and obliterating time old classic principles. Classical theories have never come to an end in roman juristic schools, and these have always been a scientific discipline not an art form or of a jigsaw puzzle notation.

The theory of diplomacy has always been understood as structure and function through substantive norms, of roman legal principles and maxims, economics is not an accepted norm in the equation of this scientific discipline of diplomacy. Economics perspectives vulgarise the very foundations of diplomacy in this regard, and several classical analogies of principles as science and diplomacy are drawn up negating vulgar concepts from economics.

CAIRO DECLARATION – CHINA AND TAIWAN – DIPOLMATIC PRINCIPLES

International diplomacy has incorporated many concepts from economics, moving it away from platonic idealistic principles. The Justification is based on money making pragmatism which fuels it. There have been theorists waiting to amend the classical principles and these are in the extensive diplomatic literature. Although there are now many instruments or tools both legal and from other disciplines, they enable understanding the legal and political arenas of intern- nation diplomacy and work most effectively when aligned to traditional internation diplomatic theories.

Diplomacy is a science a part of the legal order and underpinned by legal principles, it is practised as an art form and driven by men and women and becomes most engaged in a world of peace and conflict from which it takes the norm of a more essential mandatory activity than a privileged one.

The criticism of diplomacy is valid, diplomacy as inter nation worlds, a world of constant balancing of powers, and keeps the world stable, the Berlin wall, when demolished ended the cold war, then the union of soviet socialist republic it collapsed, world communications as the internet became dominant tool and force. The end of history and the last man can never transpire due to active, vital, vivid, tangible diplomacy. Presidents began to visit Cuba, others and shook hands with Kim Jong UN the leader of the democratic people's republic of Korea.

Great scholars entered the fray of Diplomatic inter nation summits, from the sidelines. Climate change was coined, famous scholars of the legal sciences of diplomacy gave of their time to change the world, using legal instruments on multiple forums both real and virtual, organised as diplomatic channels with key officers of the discipline of state and as private.

The modern wars frightened them out of their complacency, hybrid warfare, fought by great powers, conflicting with each others interests and promoting deadly innovative lethal weapons to do so.

In the shadows of momentous events, diplomacy entered the fray between positions of powerplays and security. Great powers became engaged, wars became the norm, nation states, began to fear each other and realism of facts on the ground, sea and air began to hit hard, the reality of global politics, and so diplomacy did not have the luxury to shy away.

There are many theorists that impact on the legal sciences of diplomacy, some theories agree on standard assumptions, others adopt them as their own. The assumption that foreign affairs as politics are inherently conflictual is not correct if legal sciences are constantly and aptly applied as precision performance. Prima facie it appears anarchy is the rule, and order, justice morality are exceptions, but the converse is the reality and with expert diplomatic applications.

Realists shrug their shoulders stating the world is anarchic but diplomacy as instrument was invented to handle chaos there is today no effective or potent central authority in international politics, it has been weakened by powerful nations. In such a disordered, dysfunctional world, nations, must guarantee, their own survival, all nations have to align with others to ensure, their survival, through the doctrine of the balancing of powers.

There are other assumptions such as the unitary system of the political sphere. Nations conflict with other nations, to share limited resources. Nations conflict with other nations, to share limited resources, and each nation follows their own interests, as natural and national interests and both can be distinguished. A national interest is above interests as specific as classification of groups individuals or politics, it represents the interest of the nation as a whole.

National interest is by far the most important concept, for neoclassicists and national interests enter their own diplomatic paradigms and are determined by only impartial rationale and reasons, and so they are not influenced by domestic policy, making processes, which interest groups influence. Political outputs are as norm shaped by the clash of interests of groups, or dominant elites and certain processes only serve these classes. Supremacy of power and security options have surfaced recently but these concepts oil become relevant with context.

The classical tradition as platonic and ideal has always sensed that international politics could become dangerous if not handled with sound precise scientifically formulated diplomacy with its inherent capacities. Moral progress can always be sifted and inconsistency, can create a problem for moral values of humans and humanity at large. Leaders must always act in accordance with set moral principles. Realism must be toned and checked by idealism, and science always disapproves as checks and balances cruel decisions made by inept and hasty politicians.

Although most schools agree with these notions and issues, albeit there are variations and different opinions on certain subset of topics. These distinctions create different models of analysis, leading to applications, of diplomacy through different processes and methods. Due to the dynamic nature and science of laws and diplomacy, different tools through specific theories as practice have emerged. These traditions are well clarified and even classified.

There is no single theory, and different theories have key focal concepts as points. Diplomacy books refer to idealism within a realist paradigm, some like to divide these even further, to classicism, neoclassicism, and realism with classicism. The analysis is wide and variants are many with many branches and sub branches.

There are many classifications as natural human nature realism as diplomacy that shaped it as one based on human nature, the other focuses on state to state behaviours as international and the internal dynamics of each enter the diplomatic paradigms as classic systems are equally important as these as concentrates impact on the behaviour of nation states.

These classifications on study inherent variations as variables and see how these impact reform, change, alter, amend renew foreign policy and they aim to understand comprehend international outcomes and individual nation states foreign policy decisions.

Questions are posed on nation states, how they gain more power or achieve national security. Their offensive and defensive poles, and how they use power as just or unjust to achieve their aims. Different paradigms as classical and realist come into play. There are many examples where scholarship on diplomacy is itself confused and these can be evaluated through different model systems.

Diplomacy feeds from different sources, and their influence becomes obvious only through its actions. The international system, works through the doctrine of the balance of power and realism and these in themselves are very extensive.

The international system does not present a clear view of the world's distinct paradigms. There are offensive structures both as theory and practice, in the international system, and these cause constant disruptions and instabilities, their roots do not stem from classical diplomacy but are inventive as structural realities created. There is no defensive against these offensive defensive modes in diplomacy, to attain peace and stability. It is crucial to realise these exist as deliberate designs.

There are many designs and they make different emphasis on realities defensive and offensive modes and feed on political realism and have many finer points at the same time and diverge from a central point. The two conflictual poles, impact human nature as deleterious and drastically alter political thought and paradigms. The norm, as ideal is that goodness rules human nature and through diplomacy based on science laws, rationality, political stability can be achieved.

In order to achieve stability, political order, rationality, and morality must be the foundational thesis of diplomacy. Mankind must apprehend substantively the problem of knowledge, deficiency and should strive to dispense with the deleterious impacts of morally inept corrupt individuals, groups and fallen corrupt institutions, albeit the world is not a faultless place and defects are inherent in all of human nature.

The Moral political order, can be achieved as interests and groups class, the best diplomatic move is to avoid conflict and address clashing and conflicting interests; albeit theorists claim the assumption that the human nature has fallen as demonian, but this is in stark contrast to classical arguments what is the cause of man's fallen nature?

There are essentially six moral ethical legal principles that dictate to diplomacy of nations, first that national and international societies are governed by natural laws and that laws as constructed stem from these and their roots arise from human nature.

Human nature is mutable, and ignoring the rise and fall of man, will have devastating impacts for diplomacy as it addresses the humanity mores of differential mankind.

In order to progress nations, human nature must be understood as mutable and effort made to develop it in a social not a political sense.

The second principle is to understand and comprehend the concept of power as nation building. The proposition, is to understand the past, present, actions of historical politicians and on this basis predict their future patterns whether they act rationally or irrationally, the theory of diplomacy does not ignore the irrationality of historical politicians.

Politics as current act in accordance with interests and these are defined as how power will be used and abused, the normative, emphasise what diplomacy ought to be. Foreign policy must be the most rational reasoned of all policies, to reduce risks and create deficiencies, as a necessity through flawed actions. The true face of diplomacy has one single aim to present a guide map to a path for bet foreign policy outputs.

There is a further point that cannot be ignored, diplomacy contains irrational inputs as manmade and these affect nations through failing policy outputs. These elements cannot be excluded from diplomatic theories, hence the theoretical presupposition is that all foreign policy is rational is untrue.

Nevertheless, these elements as irrational from diplomatic theories and hence policy, after all in terms of diplomacy, the best foreign policy will be executed by a nation with the highest IQ and the best foreign policy is often the most rational foreign policy.

Because only rational foreign policy can maximise the safety of all nation states and reduce risks that nations may face due to the application of a globalised foreign policy decision.

The third most fundamental principle of diplomacy is he concept of interest of nations, defined as power contained within them as an objective category and often not an invalid one.

These differ from time to time and place to place often it includes all actors by means either legal constitutional power or the deadly release of brutish force to decimate other nations and their peoples.

Initially the scope of this concept was narrow as a single nation went to war, with another single nation, but now the scope is as wide as possible and the means to track the actors in the globalised frameworks.

In diplomacy the relationship between morality and international diplomacy is a profound and key principle. Diplomacy emphasizes these two tensions as moral obligations demand attention such that only desirable decisions can be set forth. War as just is last resort and this concept is very strict in application. All individuals and nations have mandatory moral obligations as universal nations have no inherent right to sacrifice the lives of others on demand, and must abide by moral obligations under all circumstances, they are responsible not just for the protection of themselves as citizens but in this context not to carelessly without caution sacrifice the lives of young members of men and women at their beck and call, with prudence for life being the greatest virtue for internation political realism as diplomatic legal structures.

The fifth principle emphasizes that existence of moral criteria cannot be denied and must be used to sender diplomatic decisions as one underpinned by the highest codes and standards of moral legitimacy. All nations to fulfil their interests try to legitimise their behaviours with the moral context, for this reason, the conduct of a nation has to be evaluated by the well set established rules of moral criteria, in light of illegal power games and interest needs to promote illegal wars and must be assessed objectively and with scientific instruments.

The sixth principle of diplomacy as higher laws highlight the fact that idealism with realistic structures is autonomous from all other fields. Human nature bears many hats, dresses, labels firms as political economic foreign affairs, needs examination and should not be abstracted as only divided but as contained with the absolute human nature because only this renders man within the highest moral standards criteria.

This norm has a crucial place in diplomacy, as all politics is a struggle for power, it is a crop of dynamics of the global system, individual power is limited by society in the international sphere, there is no authority over a nation that can contain, control limits its anarchical behaviour and becomes a leviathan like very quickly.

The evil nature of man is established since prehistorical times. Nature has not made men equal either in faculties of body or mind, the inequality of personal capacities leads to distrust equality. If falsely created still does not enable man to ascend. Humans as evil will always be driven to dominate other people, so they can feel secure in themselves is a legitimate argument. They want to dominate people not because they are a threat but because they perceive themselves as inferior to them, and this unleashes the savage power as unlimited desire among mankind.

The conflictual nature of mankind even in civil states man is warring one against the other, this results in situation as undesirable consequences for all mankind. This anarchic mankind always is in charge. The future is never near or right for them.

In state of nature, man has the right to do whatsoever he wants, but nothing is safe when man is constantly seeking his goals through brute power. Man cannot dominate all people he perceives as a threat, nature disallows him, in both situations.

In order to escape this terrible human nature, man transfers his evil, to another person, or group or nation as a projection. At the end of this transfer the leviathan is the other and is constructed by him.

The state of this nature of evil man is projected into the international sphere, and so the selfishness of evil human nature is given validity, as an anarchic world unfolding through his very finger tips.

One of the reasons for this anarchy in international biosphere as law and relations is that evil man has a strong desire to overcome his inherent evil nature and cannot do this in the domestic sphere and so the anarchy ossifies at international levels.

It is vital to maintain peace in an anarchic world created by the evil man, which is not ruled by an omnipotent world state, the evil man imposes as a fraudulent model.

There are different instruments for peace, as limitations to this power, as law and norms and which can stem from any nation big or small wherever resident evil manifests as power.

Instruments are unable to maintain peace forever, one has to keep selecting the right instruments often two side b side, there is no law that demands this in nature.

Diplomats claim that a powerful state may violate international laws, rules, and moral norms. A nation states especially a powerful or dictatorial mode, complies with international law and norms, only when it serves its national interests or when it is scared of sanctions, other nation states may impose in case its actions are seen as violations of international laws. When nations like USA or Russia violate a norm, then other nation states can deter it, by the active use of the balance of power. Often international laws dispensing institutions are not trusted and are seen as weak operators under the control of the powerful nation in the globalised sphere.

Nations form alliances, within the balance of power doctrine, this is used to describe every case and every situation, and power here runs along equal lines. The international laws cover all states and aspire to maintain their status quo. There are many legal instruments mechanisms that protect the behaviour of power as a legal doctrine in the international system. The classic balance of power mechanism is an efficiency that protects and maintains peace and rests on the assumption that two superpowers and their allies have nearly equal powers and this deters wars.

The main cause of conflicts is that one side or national actor becomes more powerful than the others, and the balance of power becomes skewed shifts and becomes weaker or even is rendered desuetude, and erodes the power on one side. Often the balance of power once strengthened can also become the cause of renewed wars, if after a lengthy time, of oppression or suppression, they have enough power, to counter a revisionist attack and hence are no longer reticent to go to war, or after a period of engagement the outbreak of wars ceases and both sides avoid wars. Often the motivations of nations cannot be understood, after wars have ceased this balance of power enables the survival of small states. The importance of dominant nations cannot be denied, and the observation of human nature is important, to devise precise diplomatic policies, the theory of diplomacy within international politics, creates novel concepts as new cases and situations arise, thus taking care of the role of the accidental occurrence of unexpected events. Complete theories are impossible to formulate in light of dynamic and changing effects in peace and conflict studies.

Diplomacy can also be designed based on international outcomes which depends on the conduct of interacting units.

These must consider changes in the altering dynamics of units and international outcomes. The understanding and grasp of the concept of power is also important because of its unlimited power as nature.

Excessive armament of a state can impinge on other states, and alliances are forged for excess strengthening. Different views of anarchy must also be gasped as these create problems how nation states metabolise these and then diplomacy can create the right atmosphere for constraining conditions.

International politics and domestic politics have entirely different functioning principles, the hierarchy found in the domestic sphere with a central authority in the international systems are not centralised and hence are more anarchic. The primary aim of states is survival and to protect interests as an anarchic system. Similar status nations, have different inherent levels of power and wealth, and these are imparted, by their interacting nature and their populations.

Diplomacy tries to read international politics both through anarchy and at system levels. It concentrates not merely on the concept of power and how nations survive through anarchical periods. Powerful nations have greater ability to impact global politics but there is a caveat to this and often their power fails. Powerful states too need to survive in anarchy, and sometimes impulsion pushes them towards more aggressive behaviours within the international systems. They lose when the balance of power is restored and become vulnerable again. If they act with violence and aggression, the balance of power rises as a mechanism of laws and begins to punish them and realism becomes the root of wars again.

Diplomacy does not emphasize the benefits of conflicts for any side and its weakest point of defence is when structural realism takes shape and begins by itself to do the work of diplomacy if it has failed, and the balance of power mechanism begins to calm down the fray and pacify aggressive violent nations and states.

In diplomatic themes this argument is valid there is no need to have more power than necessary to survive. Power distributions of the future cannot be predicted and are not a stable parameter as it is always in dynamic flow within the system. The structure of power can be both benevolent for a time and can become malevolent and this impacts the entire system.

The essence of power impacts all nations in the system, the offensive conduct of nations can only be absorbed for a while this begins to change the overall dynamics of international structures rational models.

Perfect knowledge does not exist wrong decisions are related to this, analysis tools become broken, many parameters are ignored forgotten, and the new reality becomes an offensive one.

Diplomacy models never force themselves on nations if they do they become an offensive structural reality, and the converse is that defensive realism as response breaks down all structures of good, noble sound diplomacy. It is important to remind those in practice that this is the inefficiency created and shakes the bedrock of clear assumptions, the desire for hegemony becomes the nail in the coffin.

Nations have military capacities and use these as an offensive power, and these are used for attack. Even unarmed states have creative means to retaliate against an offensive nation. Nations that attack must always pre-suppose that they will be attacked, by the nation under attack. Nations need to ensure their survival; some nations may use other criteria not related to security or national security and may be simply to gain more power in the balance of power paradigm. The combination of these criteria creates general acts of nations as a result. Nations, fear powerful nations as there is no system, which can stop them, allies formed for example US and allies, but there is always intra power competition, for example UK may gain more for itself. And US may lose this power to UK, and so there are no guarantees.

All nations need to increase their power to remain safe and secure, but often surround the most powerful nation, in the system as it is the safest plan, to be in the system. A nation often does not go on the offensive, against a more powerful nation, but a powerful balanced nation in the axis will go against another powerful nation, in the axis, and have it attacked will reverse the attack of the offending nation.

Peaceful nations are rarely pleased with power and want to seize the balance of power in their favour, the geographical distribution of the world prevents nations from aligning the status of global power or hegemon, as nations are separated by vast bodies of oceans, and limit over extended power of nations.

Latent power exists in countries as specific norms unique to them, economics, wealth, popularity, population, sciences and technology, strong armies, military power. Hence military power is not the sole determinant of power. Both large populations and strong economics, are needed, to maintain a strong military force, however nations with large populations may not have strong economies, and all strong economies may not have the most powerful military force, it also depends on inherent intellect of populations, that yield superior forces through the development of the combat strategies.

The tragedy of diplomacy is that wars are fought by armies not air power, the airpower is only there to support the ground forces, even in the nuclear era. Land forces invade enemy territory, and the core function of the navy is also support but wars must only be won on land.

The other critical military issue is nuclear weapons, they have the capacity to inflict unprecedented harm, and the poles of balance even if in competition can be contained once the war is unleashed.

The breakfast of a nuclear war is always possible between two nuclear states, these weapons are not guardian angels, nor make the world safe thus all nuclear states must have land forces.

However, if a nation, develops technology, to defend itself, against nuclear attack, then it is safe from its enemies, but it must not at the same time launch a nuclear attack to show nuclear superiority, or try to be ignorant that there is no such thing as a nuclear hegemon.

The notion of power is there as a deterrent, only a miscalculation, based on imperfect information, even if irrational can lead to mistakes.

The problem of misinformation, it is seen as performance, on the battleground and war itself is a disaster and complex, the direction of war is impacted by many outcomes and factors.

In a chaotic international arena, power makes nations feel safe, island nations, have advantage over continental nations and some can abuse the powers to take control of far-off territories, and gain control over weak states. It is unlikely that landlocked nations, will ever rise thus strategy as they will soon be overcome.

Regional hegemons differ from global hegemons. Great global powers do not want other nations, to gain power and constantly try to change the balance of power.

War, blackmail, bait and bleed, bloodletting, are strategies that great powers use to change the balance of power, in their favour. Buck passing is another strategy, as he does not undertake, any responsibility or expense of war.

Like all diplomatic theories, it is important to recognise that power is a vital norm for realising good diplomacy. The notion of power is that there is latent power residing in all nations, as social strength, family, structure, as nuclear powers, support structures, strengthening family units as joint family systems, wealth, populations, sciences, philosophers, lateral deep thinking minds, reasoning power, technologies, beyond the human scope capacity and abilities, that can support persons, within armies, these non-military tech advances, humans have access to can converted to military power and strength. Military, therefore, especially in peace times, and are not needed during peace times but large populations, strong economies, can be supported, by strong armies as defence of nations. Economic power is only an indication of potential of the people to generate wealth and this depends on the size of its population. However, strong economies may nevertheless lack strong superior armies.

Might is needed to offend an enemy invading a territory, nuclear bombs do not make countries safe, they act as deterrents, reduce the possibility of the outbreak of hostilities between big powers. Cold war was fought by conventional armies, the greatest danger is that of nuclear war breaking out between two great powers, when nuclear might is no longer a guardian angel but one that will obliterate nations, even if America develops offensive tech to fend off nuclear attacks, it may not be 100 % efficient and changes are its allies could be destroyed by nuclear weapons that do have such a defence.

Power in the toolbox of diplomacy cannot be calculated efficiently and the variables of power are too may and, on this basis, imperfect calculations are made, resulting in bad decisions. The concept power of any given nation is known to all, and all nations calculate their strategies according to known power, to implement either their survival or maximise its powers.

The problem of incomplete information results in poor calculations and when there is a war to be waged, poor performance on the battlegrounds is seen. War is a complex dynamic, so many factors can alter or change the direction of a war, it is impossible to predict these accurately.

Geography in diplomacy to bring safety is important, the strongest safest nation is one separated by seas and oceans, these restrict land forces. Overseas invasions are cumbersome, some nations are insular, and others are not making them less safe. Modern warfare as in the Arabian Peninsula have begun to sue navies and air forces for warfare, thus enabling them to change the balance of power.

Diplomacy uses appeasement, to stop wars, with the multilateral powers, balance maybe impossible to attain. US wants to dominate Persia, Arabia Asia and Europe thus making it a global hegemon, power increases its sense of security, and so the envelope is pushed hard.

However, others argue that America is only a regional hegemon, as realists argue, it can be threatened by other nations, in the balance of power, axis, such as the formation of BRICS in the international system. The rise of India and China threaten America's status quo as they seek new ways to undermine the status of America through mythical modus and multiple ways.

CAIRO DECLARAION DIPLOMACY AND THE RISE OF CHINA

Nations are key actors in diplomatic international politics. They throb as the heart of the world in disparate states. The scales shift and are sensitive in international diplomacy. They rise and fall, but sometimes, an exceptional statesman can balance them all with precision performance, these are exceptionally rare as events and persons.

In this century alone, the balance as scales have gone awry many times. The wars have destabilised the scales, ruptured them. These than cause a shift in vital nodes of power centres and even dissolve them. Power is not simply wielded, through factors, as economy, socialism, but by key instruments, which can move these factors and transform them – these have been absent gone missing in the last two decades.

When China, was established in 1949, it was not a leading power, it is today. Its GDP was not as it is today, and its growth as seen from its GDP as ninety trillion in 2018/19. China rose steadily and grew by average by 8-9%., annually, the transformation was complete. These massive growth rates were due to the market economy, and a state driven system, as classical capitalist – political economic one, moving away from an age of system of pure communism.

These factors are indicators of China's rise, and equally China converted its economic power to military power, latent power, became actualised, as sufficient population entered the streams of advanced tech power, economic power and military power and might.

China continues on its upward trajectory and is now considered an industrial giant. China unleashed its military spending taking a giant leap to 252.4 billion from just twenty-five billion in just a short period of time. However, it cannot be dismissed, that China is still a developing country with enormous growth potential.

CAIRO DECLARATION DIPLOMACY AND CHINA'S ECONOMIC ASCENSION

China's economic ascendance cannot be easily understood.

Early days -

This is not the first rise of China, it was one of the wealthiest nations in the past, but in the 17th-18th centuries Europe in the west had surpassed China in both sciences and per capita wealth, UK rise due to its colonization of India in the 18th century and thus Western Europe rose along with it. It received boundless resources from its colonies and reached a level of power unprecedented in the world. Military power defeated China in 1860, and many concessions in foreign trade followed. China became part of Britain's integrated capitalist system. China accepted unwillingly the independence of Korea, lost Ryukyu islands and had to pay war indemnities to Japan. Many rebellions followed as the boxer, Wuchang and the Qing dynasty fell and was replaced by the republic of China.

China was divided and was ruled by war lords, the communist party then emerged, and Japan entered World War II, on the side of the axial power. Japan withdrew from China.

MID-DAYS DIPLOMACY

China became a unitary state but had an underdeveloped poor economy. China controlled commerce and changed into a central commercial system and production was the remit of the government. Private sector did not exist, then came the cultural revolution, and ideology, surfaced as political and economics. There was much suffering and upheaval, China had little to no influence over the world, politics. Often powers determine how nations engage with international relations, then it was seen as a developing nation. New rulers like Deng Xiaoping began reforms and turned China around. The reforms resulted in liberalisation, agriculture reforms and others, which expanded into economic enterprises, became fruitful.

One of the most critical points was the Russian revolution, social disintegration was inevitable, China was forced to rise.

NEW ERA DIPLOMACY

With Mao's death, Xiaoping rose, to power and collective business gave rise to effective tools, to transform, the economy and outputs began to increase by 20 percent annually, and the economy began to expand exponentially.

Government changed its model and decision-making capacities control centres began to loosen their grip, and production and innovation became the norm. Five-year developmental plans began to move, assess, performance and evaluate the changes and medium sized companies began to flourish and the economy as private was realised and given legal status. China implemented further changes as open door and foreign investment began to flood in. Flexibility resulted in ownership if firms and controls on import and export were relaxed. Exports were supported by the nation states and foreign investments rose from one billion to thirty billion in just a few years.

The FDI began to generate more than 50% of the GDP of China, and multinationals came into China and foreign trade was in full flow. China began to exhibit traits of a market economy, and China denounced the methods suggested by IMF, world bank and Washington and instead created its own privatisation method, and non-state sector began to grow and became production, import, export was managed by the floating exchange rates system, and Beijing began to participate in the WTO, this made foreign trade free of restricting protectionist measures and China officially entered the world market.

It was as if a new epoch had begun scholars suggested that China would overtake US by 2035, and become the largest economy in the world, China was on its way to become the world's second largest economy, with a large population, and large military spending.

DIPLOMACY RELATIONSHIPS OF CHINA DURING ITS ECONOMIC AND MILITARY RISE.

Economic growth is only one indicator of development as measured by GDP and income levels, and equally how a nation invests in education, infrastructure and on health and other expenses. Defence too is important. The world economy is gradually shifting from west to east and SIPRI announced that China's military expenditure has increased over the last few decades, and China began to modernise its politics, it studied various models around the world, including the US war in Iraq, and inserted high tech into its warfare conditions, NATO's war in Yugoslavia was also due to technological superiority. China began to transport equipment, personnel, and prioritised tech intensive structures, function, and competition. Command and leadership changed, and simulations were created for strengthening Navy, army, and air force. The Navy spending rose, and destroyers were increased nuclear submarines, were entered into the equation and China converted its latent power into a military power. China's navy now had the capacity to launch amphibious landings and threatened US bases in Philippines and Guam and its dominance over the south China sea grew, its radars, anti-air missile batteries increased the power projection of China in the region of the Chinese seas but also internationally.

The air force with its role in supporting ground operations and inflicting damage in conflict zones was modernised sufficiently and field work began on warning systems, and attacks defence and offence and their scope was contained, reshuffling of structures and functions began in dead earnest. China has the largest aviation inventory, nearly three thousand aircraft, many warplanes, fighters ground attack aircraft and other military aircraft, many warplanes, fighters, ground attack aircraft and other military aircraft. Chinese air force has increased with growing economic power, artificial intelligence, quantum computer systems, autonomous systems, biotechnology systems form part of Chinese military strategies and surveillance systems and reconnaissance, warning systems, along with navigation satellites.

This capacity has only increased as deterrents against China's growing number of enemies and can be used for offensives against them.

Unmanned vehicles as used in wars help to transport good to wounded soldiers and technological superiority was a must for China.

China has nuclear weapons too and they have increased their warning and reaction capacities to deter nations. Nuclear submarines have capacity to attack an aggressive nation with nuclear weapons.

Effect on China on international system, the effect of China's rise on the international system.

China's modernisation has had a lot of impact on international systems, and relation, as it, continues to grasp cyber space weapons and fields. In this sense China has enormous capacity against external threats. All these stems from its rise and often it conflicts with American interests in the Asia Pacific.

The republic wants to sustain a wealthy and powerful nation, and it has national security concerns, as attacks from other nations but has no desire for power over other countries, China is not interested in Hegemony.

USA is not a regional hegemon, in the region and can be easily pushed out, as its bases are based in the pacific. This dualism stems from the uncertain nature in diplomatic relations and China will want stable Chinese seas, free from American aggressive presence, the most powerful nation, in the region. The dangerous nature of diplomatic international relations is contained when a superpower exists among them. This is the general theoretical framework and as China becomes the hegemon, it will serve as protector of weaker nation, and this will enable to rise in the sphere along with China.

As Chinese economy grows it will transform its populations and those of the Koreas, Taiwan, and Japan, with technological and shared industrial growth.

The weakening of the USA in its own sphere, with NATO nations, Arab, Asian nations. Russian nation implies it will no longer be the regional hegemon, in the Chinese seas. Regional oriental hegemon will not endeavour to hinder the emergence of others as hegemon, nor will it be afraid, of competing interests.

International diplomacy will change as a result in this region, but also reducing power of US as an imported hegemon into this region. It will be inevitable that US will not be able to hold out against China as a regional hegemon. US will be pushed out and will try to maintain its hegemon. Atlantic sphere but will not be permitted to do so in the pacific sphere, composed mainly of oriental races and nations.

China will become the most powerful in its region and Asia Arabia pacific nations will have their own code of balance of power in this region. China will not cede Taiwan under international laws entrenched as far back as the Cairo Declaration, set in Egypt to restore Taiwan, safely as a united and One China.

The Belt and road initiative is one of the biggest paradigms that China has developed, China has islands in the South China Sea.

DIPLOMACY AS CAIRO DECLARATION THE TAIWAN AND CHINA ONE NATION.

TAIWAN DIPLOMACY

The outbreak of the Ukraine Russian war meant that peace protocols had to be activated under international laws, and they were by Italy and China on the Crimea question, which has powerful connections with Russia. USA then began to focus on China and Taiwan, trying to divide them as a single polity. Taiwan legal status is not a controversial one, its fate like the west and east Germany was divided but the Cairo declaration as ratified so no confusion arises has stated it belong to China. Taiwan is Chinese by origins and connections, as historical and the sovereignty of China, rules both China and Taiwan, post world wars. Illegal migrations began from Japan and Korea, and its population grew to twenty-four million, but America supported, its division rather than union by history. Other powers as major do not follow the American stance. It is not recognised as an independent nation, in its own right. Its union with China is obstructed post Cairo Declaration by USA.

Taiwan has 36,197 square kilometres of land, it consists of Taiwan, Kinmen Matsu, and other islands in the South China sea. It has a multi-party democratic system, its economy has been developed by America, and it has a high GDP and is also highly developed technology power, artificial intelligence, and internet.

It is not an obstacle to its union as complete with China, and tough international law factors. Taiwan is by these and laws Chinese.

CAIRO DECLARATION AND THE TAIWAN QUESTION.

The root of the Taiwan question begins with Imperial China, which was the sovereign of the Pescadores islands, close to Formosa Island which is mainland Taiwan. It did not control Formosa Island, and in the 17th century Japan and Spain tried to take over the islands. However, under Law of oceans, its attachment as Taiwan as connecting factors is greatest to China. The Dutch too tried to take over the island after the Qing dynasty followed the Ming dynasty -Chinese began to migrate to the Formosa Island, and so the island became inhabited by mainland Chinese in 1661. Qing dynasty was in control and not the Ming dynasty. The island was then under the direct control of the island and the notion it belonged to the Dutch, Spanish, or Japanese was rendered null and void as hostile takeover invaders into Chinese oceans.

A Sino Japanese war was fought, and the Japanese used brute force to take over the island and this lasted for a while, till the world wars started and Japan was forced to withdraw from Taiwan and the island once more came under China's sovereignty. The Cairo declaration followed shortly after world wars and its signatories were America and England now USA and UK, but in 1983, and so Taiwan was declared the sovereign state of China and Japan was ousted and rendered as occupier null and void. Chinese leader Chiang Kai Shelk was a signatory to the declaration as leader of China. Japan was dismissed as illegal usurper of the island.

China won over Japanese in the second world war, a civil war resulted in withdrawal or lack of control of the island, but once civil war ended Maso regained control of Taiwan and the islands.

US during the outbreak of the Korean war, tried to overturn Taiwan using its 7th fleet in 1950 under President Truman, but this was deemed illegal invasion by China. Taiwan was part of China and China had no strategy to protest the hostile takeover of Taiwan by US 7th fleet, and it came a shock that US had taken advantage of the hostile takeover of Taiwan port its civil war and the armed forces of China, their stopping power, and the water located between mainland China and Taiwan played a role in preventing such a hostile bold takeover of sovereign island Taiwan by the US under President Truman.

China post 1953 began to take Taiwan back, but America played a defence treaty with Taiwan thus reclaiming as its own to defend. The Taiwan strait crisis deepened and the Dachen, Tyi Anshan islands were freed from American control albeit using Taiwan as its excuse. As a result, the Formosa resolution was adopted to strengthen the defence treaty of America and Taiwan islands.

Later another Taiwan crisis began and for America and China made a new attempt to take back its island Taiwan, but US sent nuclear weapons to Taiwan, with five aircraft carriers the nuclear capable B47 bombers were used on Guam, but China did not stop to take back Taiwan out of American control. The US then placed nuclear weapons again and threatened China it would use the nuclear weapons and reasserted Taiwan under its control and defence structures.

China represented Chinese people in Taiwan legally at the United Nations. The UNGA influenced by US passed resolution 2758 to make China null and void as sovereign of Taiwan, as per Cairo declaration and prior historical history as ancient and modern with various land connecting factors and expelled it from the UN but China gained a seat with the UNGA and it also became one of the five permanent members of UNSC. This undermined Taiwan in global politics, and undermined American interference in China's domestic affairs.

In 1972 America post this event, began to warm its relations with China, and Taiwan China became the status quo. Under President Carter America terminated its defence treaty and asserted the PRC of Taiwan would gain full recognition, while China, would lose it averse to its legal rights, as sovereign and under the much talked about Cairo declaration. Both moves by America further endangered the China Taiwan status quo as well as Taiwan security.

Later congress in America adopted a Taiwan relations Act in 1979, and a new legal framework was used to manage the relation with Taiwan, which US did not recognise. It was to promote trade between Taiwan and US while maintaining peace and stability in the region. US also committed to supply arms to Taiwan.

China considers Taiwan its own, and rejuvenation protocols are underway to reignite this programme of reunification.

Throughout history, Power has risen in different places, like Germany, USA, Soviet Union, and often these have tried to expand into their surrounding regions often with limited success as defence offence structures come into play and these exist as a historical rule towards all rising power, China may not be an exception, as a general principle stronger nations feel more secure then weaker nations, and all need to feel safe in an anarchic world of international politics.

The current world crisis is one which China is getting stronger than most other nations. It desires to transform other nations like its model that are lagging behind, in economic and military strength. The argument for offence, structural realms have failed thus far to suggest that China is seeking global and regional hegemony. China has not followed aggressive policies thus far and back a win win situation in the regions and globally in the future. China's policies are firm and accepted by all nations. Taiwan belongs to China under the paradigm of international laws, history, connections, population, and firm ratified treaties. Thus, it is wrong for detractors to state that China has a desire for hegemony, whilst its arguments are based on the roman maxim, first in right is stronger in might but aggressive nations towards China state that China has aims for hegemony citing Taiwan wrongly under established laws.

Assertive and dominant nations like USA have often post the world wars created controversies over Taiwan, with its neighbouring states, but China, has never used an aggressive attitude towards these nations, thus in this context, China's model cannot be analysed in light of offensive realism of rising nations, seeking hegemony. China's stance towards Taiwan is national security oriented as it sees Taiwan as legally its own since the end of world wars and its uses offensive structures as realistic towards aggressive nations who wish to tear Taiwan away from China and thus occupying it legally and illegally.

China's modernisation programmes, emphasises the same in regional regions as mentioned at its SCO summit meetings and its military security has increased and been enhanced since its rise in power.

China regularly conducts military programmes to protect Taiwan, but USA has marked it as its own and states that China is violating Taiwan's air defences, but these manoeuvres are simply to prevent USA's expansionist claims over other into China regions which includes Taiwan as legally owned by China, USA creates through its influence since the Cairo declaration, Taiwan, that China should be deemed a threat as perception, and this has permeated through its influence into common Taiwan, structures and society. USA has assured Taiwan, that China fighter aircraft may soar closer and begin an operation, to hit Taiwan, but due to international laws and relations, China will abstain for its honour's sake. However, China viewpoint is diametrically opposed to its enemy's stance, which USA under international laws, is, China, offers states that USA is out to divide both China and Taiwan and that its furtive intentions are never clear. China on the other hand has never renounced its reunification policy under the ratified treaty and as past and present laws.

Taiwan had illegal migration from Japan, Marilyn and thus these were in turn supported by USA to create secession under international laws from China. However China moved quickly recognising foreign interference from Japan and USA and swiftly passed an anti-secession law and also cited the casus belli for Taiwan's illegal declaration of independence goaded on by USA and thus Taiwan's illegal declaration of independence goaded on by USA, and thus Taiwan has no option under laws to be one with China, or else be a vassal state of USA under its protections, as military or to go independent would mean this as it has virtually no military power of its own.

China is aware that it must place pressure on USA through the international community, to prevent its interference, in its initial affairs, and in Taiwan to reunify in a stronger way shedding all its interference in both national affairs.

Taiwan has repeatedly been occupied by foreign nations. China has quickly grown to the second largest economy in the world, and Taiwan knows this. Separatist forces infiltrated Taiwan a long time ago and prevent a One China policy. China is committed to this policy and desires for a reunification as peaceful but would use free as it knows foreign nations are aiming to prevent this and as last reset. China has modernized its army and reshaped its structures and functions, replaced od weapons, modernised nuclear weapons and gained more battleships and planes and also the new generation of tech weapons. These will be used to regain Taiwan if all peaceful means fail due to resistance groups.

The USA is concerned about China's growing capacity, if US has to intervene in a war, it will have to be cautious and China its expanding power capacity, is revealed by its concepts of science, it has revealed as papers. Diplomatic resolution is the safest way for power projection and to control the various claims. These islands start from the southern coasts of Japan and expand outwards to the Philippines, and Malaysian coasts and then onto Taiwan.

The second islands include Manana Island Palam, Guam, and they are effective in open oceans. China's capacity is noninterfering on the islands, and it sees no norm to contain Japan or Korea, Philippines, Malaysia, Vietnam, or Taiwan, as oceans recede, China's power threatens US presence in the Pacific Ocean. It has also been emphasized that island chains have both diplomatic overseeing from China, but US presence requires China to develop its weapon systems to keep it at bay. China's protections over the seas are increasing and it has the largest navy, and its battleship production is at par with the USA; whilst also improving its operations and also reshuffling its troops. Thus, it can depend on neighbouring states, its mainland interests in the sea and intervene if attacked by US mobility and power in the Asia pacific region. China presents USA to become a regional hegemon. China extends over the South China sea, and its policies to protect Taiwan and far ranging China, overseas, Spratly islands, and has bases to protect it from the USA, it is enlarging its reefs by landfilling, and making sure there are no active threats, present near its airstrips, preventing US military projection over its regional states. China, Vietnam, Philippines, Indonesia, Malaysia, Brunei, all claim some of the islands in the oceans and China too does the same, over many of its reefs. There are many historical sites in the region, and Malacca strait is rich in oil and its energy needs. Reunification is both an economic strategy for China as well as deemed as a legal right of China. Taiwan stands tall over the sea lanes, of eastern China and Asia and is a major point of world trade, and its coastal areas are vulnerable to US attacks from its bases in Taiwan. China reasserts its power over Taiwan and control its economic resources, capital by importing all its goods, products its twenty-four million populations and so Taiwan's produce increases China's economic power, and China's legal expectations on Taiwan rest on the fact and bases of the Cairo treaty and declaration its key points as legal. As far as China goes, the legal position is already ratio decidendi, rejected by those averse to China's interests, to prevent Taiwan and equally China from becoming an economic power. US is trying to modernise Taiwan's army and teaching it asymmetric warfare strategies against China, and this intervention as military threatens China. It constantly approves the sale of weapons in large quantities and maintains its relationship with it and will support Taiwan and even encourage it in a conflict with China.

As China surpasses USA economically, in technology, military and other key areas, US worries about the power China will reach in the future and US perplexed has placed its bases in the Asia pacific region and uses them in overseas geographics. US thus could attack China from these bases and also use its allies to do the same in the region, US uses Taiwan to make legitimate its interventions in the Taiwan Strait and increases its sales to it and other nations. All these clearly show, that the relationship between China and Taiwan is an acrimonious one, all this may change if Russia and China combine their strength and attack the USA. The international system thus is dominated by US bases and thus it creates safety for itself as a nation. US in the past 240 years has only ceased from war for a mere 16 years thus providing the rise of the regional hegemons and thus contains rising powers like China.

China is the next powerful nation in its reign today – there is in its region today – There is no balance of power and USA threatens China's national security and its anti-stance towards China Taiwan policy is a skewed perspective, it disrupts the close relations between China Taiwan as under national laws.

US dominant put pressure on China and prevents it from becoming the dormant power in the region and the world. The expats China to imitate America by following unilateral aggressive policies and dominate nations, annex their territories this is highly unlikely. China adds diplomatic relationship and supports these through white papers.

China asserts Taiwan is part of its country and that this is unique to it, but that America has instantly interfered and opposed it. USA knew China Taiwan together will result in a much stronger China and prevents this by all nations,

Taiwan and China are key to its rise and US uses offensive structural realism to project its aggressive policies to contain China through Taiwan.

The Belt and road initiative, support trade development, with collaborating nations and serves its rise and growth towards becoming a super dominant power.

CHINA'S NOVEL DIPLOMACY AS BELT AND ROAD DIPLOMACY

American authors see China through the lens of world politics and hegemony often through fear and anxiety and that if China rises it will swing the balance of power, in an already anarchical system. USA sees that China will disrupt the delicate balance in trade sphere, and hence power and the world. In their equation on the failure realise the internal politics and other unique features about China. China's rise mimics that of Russia, Germany Japan, and the USA. All of these nations share common characteristics in their trajectory to super states and powers. As Indo pacific states fear China as a risen nation, and it will be the most disruptive threat in the world, according to the American authors they deem that the most important determinant of China's power will be its military power, but equally economic power, China has increased its defence budget, but also it has altered the balance of power in favour of itself and historical evidence of rising nation that the system on which it is based dictate the rules upon which it rises. Its foreign policy when analysed indicates the arguments of structural concepts, align with China's policies towards keeping its legal rights as the Cairo declaration, active and as high politics by legal political, military economic and security drives. A single policy like the foreign policy impacts all other policies contained in Chinese government toolbox and hence the impact it has on domestic international politics makes it key to arrive at the right conclusions.

The road moves from China to Gwalior, Singapore, through Greece, Italy to Netherlands – the oceanic lanes start from China and pass through Sri Lanka Djibouti, Egypt, Belgium, Nigeria, Dubai, Kenya, Singapore to Peru, the economic strength of nations lie along these. OECD reports state that energy, resource planes, crisis cross through here and pass near Eurasia land Bridge – railway line from which runs from China to Europe, it along the way also passes through Kazakhstan, Belarus, eastern Europe, it along the way also passes through Kazakhstan, Belarus, Eastern Europe, Russia then another one connects China, Mongolia to Russia and finally China to Iran and Turkey, into India is the fourth one includes Laos, is the fourth one includes Laos, Malaysia, Kenan mar, Thailand and Vietnam. Thus most of the world's regions and connected, and a final one connects China, Pakistan, bringing in the ports of Xinjiang and Gwardar – this in itself is a major undertaking and constitutes the silk and belt road, used primarily for military economic reasons, recently China expanded it in scope and included India, Burma, (Myanmar) and Bangladesh as well and the scope of the projects intended to even connect key highways with major railways. The oceans include South China sea, Indian Ocean, Arabia, Persian Gulf red sea and Mediterranean seas.

The world falls into its lap as a major framework, Egypt, Africa, overt nations, North Africa, Latin America New Zealand, Koreas, southern Africa, from pacific oceans to the Baltic seas.

Thus, a very large trade line is created with distinct geographies. The energy infrastructure of various nations loops in and out, as well as project Arabia, Middle East, and the strait of Malacca, multilateralism is important and multilateral financial institutions have been created already roads, railways bridges, damns, power grids, have been built in one seventy nations. Grants are available for many projects, this then is a novel diplomatic initiative since the post-world war marshal plan, it touches the lives of over four million people and a third to half of the world's wealth systems.

The initiative will further world peace and will shut down or phase out offensive structure function, paradigms as wars for gain or great power competition, China remains the centre of the world. Economics is a crucial component for furthering peace. China intends to be the world's second largest spender on military growth and development. Will China like USA wants to establish regional and global hegemony, is a discourse that can be built and its foreign policy and silk belt road initiative.

Xi Jinping lauds the initiative as akin to the old silk road initiative it is the biggest budget over assigned to foreign policy. The Ministry of foreign affairs see it as the only peace cooperation transparency, leading for growth and education as well as enhancing the mutuality doctrine. The connecting lanes will foster harmony among diverse civilizations. The silk road is seen as the common thread of all civilizations.

The silk road aims to integrate many continents as Europe, Arab- Asia, Africa, and Latin America, the romance of the silk road cannot be denied, these payments will equally provide economic growth for all nations, participating oil pipelines gas pipelines, highways, transportation, lines, we'll all be part of the projects and there are positive implications for all participating nations, and the positive feedback loops that will be created will be towards world peace, and progress. Unimpeded trade will be part and parcel of the initiative, and forestry, climate, safe agricultural maritime, fishing ocean projects all will be included. Exploration of fossil fuels will be increased to find alternative energy resource, grants favourable financing will be part as national development, underpinned by reform laws.

China also asserts that bonds between different cultural civilizations will strengthen as a result as stated by Chinese reform commission chapter IV student exchange programmes.

China's key to success lies in being the benevolent index for all humanity and enhancing the felicia index and shifting its scale to the positive side of it. At this point and time economically China as power, is in direct competition with the USA, its only rival on the global scale. Certain nations as critical of China as not being inclusive with only 147 participating states, studies show that many of China's neighbours have not signed a memorandum of understanding and so the relationship as contractual commercial diplomatic is not clear and certain. Russia however is the closest ally of China both in the economic corridors but equally diplomatic and militarily.

Neighbouring states clamour that these will be the most negatively impacted by China's rise as a hegemon and also due to the irrational scenarios that exist between neighbours. Balance of power will not decrease China's power as the balance of power depends on many factors and China's rise is due to these unique factors. China's reasonability harks back to the roman jurisprudence and Augustinian thought where nation building and civilizing peoples increased Rome's power as benevolent, by enabling neighbouring nations and building for them roads, bridges, energy lines, ports and now railways The mind set of classic Rome as first five was not designed for war, these came in from non-roman citizens who usurped Rome down twenty or more dynasties. The arguments for were thus fails under this model, China and Russia have stuck to classic paradigms not modern inventive ones as lesser norms, which they attribute to their success in peace conflict and as diplomacy. Economic development, therefore, with the propagation of peace does not have to lend itself to its military might as offensive but merely as a defensive structure.

Is China, then the ancient Classic Rome, rising out of the ashes of the wars of two decades. Chinese financial institution will provide loans to nations and as many lack the financial means. Thus, participating nations will have to comply with China's banking system and rules. The Projects cover many multidisciplinary fields, and supports nations at all levels, and inadvertently it will enhance China's role in global politics and hence diplomacy. The global financial crisis of 2008 slowed down China in 2012, as China's financial model is based on export-oriented paradigm and due to cheap labour and market demands in Asian and western nations, was considerably less. China tried to activate the domestic market, but this failed due to the habits of people and systems of China as society did not help to increase production capacity.

Equally transport connections in China regions were lacking to drive the domestic initiative; China turned to infrastructure of developing nations, and also introduced the developed high-speed railways. These alternative processes were done during the slump in the international market.

India and Russia other great powers in the pacific regions, participated but complain of inadequate balance with China, and the hindrances caused to the growth by its protectionist measures. China leverages its economy especially by giving Iran to developing countries, but these loans can equally by giving Iran to developing countries, but these loans can equally lead nations into serious debt problems. Loans or aid given to nations often makes the recipient nation vulnerable to influence.

Contract loans favour China and failure to pay enables China to change focus and policies with debtor state, thus making China's influence, grow in the region.

China continues to enlarge its islands, as well as equipping them with military facilities. The foreign office of ASEAN states has objected to China building military bases on these islands.

In into pacific region, US still holds influence and China has to seek its mobility in other economic corridors. US holds military bases with its allies in the Indo pacific region with naval bases, some with absolute superiority on the seas. US tries to curb China's rise using policies and also prevents it from keeping good relations with its neighbours, it regularly has ambitious projects with Philippines and Japan and tries to intervene intentional disputes and on the other hand it disrupts good relations between its neighbours and China.

China's diplomatic relations with USA deteriorated with USA over arms supply to Taiwan.

CHINA EU EUROPE AND THE BELT AND ROAD DIPLOMACY

Most international trade is done over ocean lines, and maritime channels, are used for export imports of materials. Strategy plays a vital role in all economic and diplomatic protocols. Energy sufficiency is a problem for all nations, but China is the largest importer of gas and oil, some arrive from the Malacca strait, others from the middle east and Russia. Thus, with BRI China will increase its trade and the world and also its energy needs.

The Port of Gwadar (Indian Ocean) connects to the Persian Gulf – and is used for import of oil from the Middle East Arabian nations. State owned companies are also doing business with strategic ports in Malaysia, other areas of strategic importance to China.

Gwadar port has larger maritime vessels of China and the point and principle of these is that China could use it as well as a political and military strategy.

USA is a dominant power, and it dominates regions of the world with its national power.

The idea of defensive and offensive structures build by nations is to give them a sense of security and power. US naval projection is more powerful in the Indo pacific region, such that it can launch offensives anywhere in the world.

China has increased its naval might and capacity by establishing more robust overseas structures.

China wants to regain Taiwan, lost by foreign neglect, rejections of the Cairo Declaration, and equally by interference, in its domestic affairs.

The success of the BRI will erode the influence of Russia and USA as well of India in the Indo pacific region and will serve to bolster the strength and power of China.

SUMMA THE CAIRO DECLARATION CHINA AND TAIWAN

According to diplomatic protocols and promoting peace and welfare in an otherwise anarchical system in China can only do this using BRI as structure function but to do this well it must be the most powerful nation in the Indo Pacific and also the safest. There can be no two kings on a hill, but in the balance of power, axis it has always been US, allies, Russia, and allies, with reference to peace, war, and diplomacy, to keep the east safe from the aggressors of the west towards it. In terms of economic power USA leads nations and others follow in the west. If China becomes an economic power, the power axis will shift to the east and pacific from the west and the Atlantic nations. This will have the high impact of USA being replaced by China and its nations as the Indo pacific would rise above those of USA and the Atlantic nations which comprise the west. Within the scope of this essay, it has been evaluated that once Taiwan China are one, as per the dictates and legality of the Cairo declaration, then the BRI initiative as novel diplomacy protocol and business, will swing the balance of power, from western nations to the eastern nations, including Russia. If China's policies are sound the change could occur very quickly. China's modernization, plan includes all areas, not simply economic, but military and diplomatic as well.

China now spends more on its military spending, than all nations, put together, in the Indo pacific as far as Russia. China is also pursuing policies to reduce the power and influence in the Indo pacific region, strengthening its land, armies, acquiring air power, and ships in its military inventory. Technology is the new generation warfare and cutting-edge systems as AI warring systems and spyware. Nuclear retaliation remains last resort, and China has issued another declaratory, to enforce the original act of law, the Cairo declaration and that Taiwan emphasis remains as legal that it is part of China, and its simplicity is morally and legally right and lies in the sovereign hands of China. The stalemate remains between the west and east and China reverts time and again to the Juristic position that has not been eroded by time under international laws and relations This equally has the impact of limiting intensive aggressive stances from the USA and her allies, mainly NATO nations. China increased its activity in the East China seas, and USA accused it as averse to standing laws that China was violating the norms of

Taiwan, which is maintained by a military force as USA and thus is under its dominion as nation state. China's rebuttal has been made clear at the United Nations, and it has intensified its diplomatic measures to retain its full legal sovereignty over its islands mainly Taiwan.

In light of other points, it is clear, that the One China Taiwan paradigm with BRI will ensure and establish the rise of China and increase its powers regionally and globally. The beginning of the virtuous cycle will be established by China itself and no other as the sovereign of both China and Taiwan its indigenous part and indivisible.

REFERENCES

http://www.nytimes.com/2018/06/25/world/asia/china-sri-lanka-poet.html.

http://www.taiwan.gov.fw.about.php

http://www.mfa.gove.cn/ce/cebe/eng/zt/gs/t187130.htm.

Atesoglu, H.S., (2013) Economic growth and military spending in China: implications for international security. International Journal of Political economy, (42), pp88-100.

Benit, E (1978), Growth and defence in developing countries economic development and cultural change, 26(2), pp 271-280.

Burchill, S and Linklater, A (Eds), (2013) Theories of international relations (fifth ed), Palgrave, Macmillan.

Cardona T., D.J., (2019\0 China in Latin America -An inconvenient guest OA SIS, 30 pp 77-96.

http://www.wefonew.org/agenda/2015/09/4-ways-totackle-china's overcapacity - problem.

Ding A.S., (2019), The people's liberation Army and China's Taiwan policy under Xi Jinping: One Joint actor without its own agenda. In R.A. Bitzinger & J. Char (Eds). Rehaping the Chinese military, the PCA's roles and missions in the Xi Jinping Era (pp45-65). Routledge.

Elman.C. (1996a). Horses for courses – why not neorealist theories of foreign policy? Security studies 6 (1) pp 7-53.

Fallon T (2015). The New Silk Road: Xi Jinping's grand strategy for Eurasia. American foreign policy interests, 33 (3), pp 140-147.

Hancock K.J., Alobell, S.T. (2010). Realism and the changing international system: Will China and Russia challenge the status quo? China and Eurasia forum quarterly, 8(4)., 143-165.

Hobbes, T, (1998) Leviathan, Oxford University Press.

Junxian, G., and Yan, M (2016), China's new silk road, where does it lead? Asian Perspective, 40 (1) pp 105-130.

Krishner, J (2009) Realist political economy: Traditional themes and contemporary challenges. In M Blyth (Eds), Routledge Handbook of International political economy (IPE): IPE as a global conversation (pp36-47), Routledge.

Layne, C., (2006) – The peace of illusions, American grand strategy from 1940 to the present Cornell University Press: Ithaca and London.

Layne.C (2012) This time is real, the end of unipolarity and the Pax Americana International studies quarterly,56, pp 203-213.

McCready, D. (2003) Crisis deterrence in the Taiwan Strait. Strategic studies, institute US Army war college.

Mearsheimer, J J (2014 a), America unhinged, the National interest, (129), pp 9-30.

Ministry of foreign affairs of the people's republic of China. (2022, Aug 5). The Ministry of foreign affairs, announces, counter measures in response to Nancy Pelosi's visit to Taiwan.
Http://wwwfmprc.gove.cn/eng/zxxx-662805202208/t20220805-10735706.html.

National Bureau of statistics of China (NBS) (n.d) National data: National Government revenue and expenditure. Retrieved November 19, 2022 from: https://data.stats.gov.ca/English/tablequery.htm?code=ACO7

OECD Business and financial outlook (2018) China's belt and road initiative in the global trade, investment and Finance, landscape. Retrieved September 22. 2022, from https://www.oecd.org/finance/china-belt-and-road initiative-in the global-trade-investment-and finance--landscape.pdf.

Rabbani, A (2019), China's Hegemony in the South China Sea, world affairs. The journal of international issues, 23(3), pp, 66-79.

Taliaferro. J.W. (2000) Security seeking under anarchy: defensive realism revisited. International security, 25 (3) pp 128-161.

Toft P, (2005) John J Mearsheimer: An offensive realist between Geopolitics and Power, Journal of international relations and Development 8pp 381-408.

Zhay Z (2018). The Belt and road initiative: China's New geopolitical strategy? China quarterly of International strategic studies, 4(03) pp 327-343.

ABOUT THE BOOK

The Once China Taiwan thesis, stems from the Cairo declaration ratified post world wars.

The post-world war status and jurisdiction over Taiwan and its appertaining islands including Penghu were further ratified under various legal instruments, post the Cairo Declaration, Potsdam proclamation, Japanese instrument of surrender, the San Francisco, Peace Treaty and Treaty of Peace under the republic of China and Japan of 1952. The implementation of the legal obligation to return Taiwan and its appertaining island (including the Diaoyutai islands) to the ROC were first stipulated in the Cairo declaration and later reaffirmed in the Potsdam proclamation, the Japanese instrument of surrender, the San Francisco treaty, and the treaty of Peace between the republic of China and Japan. The Cairo declaration thus is singularly the most important legal instrument ratified post world wars and is a binding as laws.

ABOUT THE AUTHOR

Dr Amrit Rattan K Baidwan Macfarland primarily trained as a scientist, as molecular geneticist and as professor (lecturer and academician, at her universities Scots and American as secondments) and taught undergraduates and post graduates, major sciences as well as collaborated on major projects involving the subjects of Physics, cell membrane genetics, signal and transduction mechanisms in multiple biological systems, and spent time in home universities and in the USA mainly Jefferson Medical University, National Institutes of Health, Bethesda; Indiana University School of Medicine and sciences, and in institutions Sloane Kettering New York and Washington State. She went on many exchange visits as professor, teaching research methods and taught extensively molecular genetics and biomedical sciences. She has many articles, reviews and papers in peer reviewed journals and travelled widely across the globe to present her first seminal findings as first author or only author as chief scientific researcher in, cancer biology, blood brain barrier signalling methods, chondrocyte and soft tissues research at International conferences in Europe, USA, Middle East and far East, winning many prestigious scholarships, and named fellowships to conduct university business in many nations in the world as also science diplomacy for her university department/s. She worked closely with her law school, on collaborative science - law projects to assimilate her ideas as IP, patents/technology and copyright regulatory issues with her four major research lies. Her result grew in laws, and she trained as a lawyer with law firm/s having obtained a first in her dissertation as Masters in laws. Her legal knowledge in international relations, peace, and conflict studies, studied with Juris Doctors as summa cum laude from Harvard, Princeton, Washington, Cornell, Yale universities, as undergraduate, serves as a foundation for her books on major contemporary living history from the date 9/11 to the present and ongoing.

PROLOGUE

Commissioning THE YOUNG DIPLOMATS OF THE FUTURES - contemporary living history as war and peace 2001 – present

"In exile a righteous diplomat serves with pluck and courage."

Diplomats of Time, Senior Commander of the Indian Navy as diplomat to the USA with President Eisenhower (world wars I and II) B S Ranjit

Senior Commander /Captain of Off Shore Ocean Operations, Aviator, Veteran, Flight Safety Operations Global Holland, EU and Africa, Captain M G Macfarland

Painting by Captain M G Macfarland of Mahatma Gandhi (THE GREAT, only Noble One of Indus civilization) Barrister in laws and chief protagonist, not unlike Napoleon Bonaparte Dauphin of France, who destroyed the unholy roman empire (not classic Rome) a conglomeration of European nations, he was the prime directive as Barrister, Lawyer whose passive movement (Satyagraha a Sanskrit word moving in truth and veritas) and legal arguments resulted in the liberation of India, and the fall of the British Empire, around the world, as Adolf Hitler of Germany commenced the world wars, I and II against all of the European lands including the isles of Britain, once subjected to Roman laws and rulers.

www.ingramcontent.com/pod-product-compliance
Lightning Source LLC
LaVergne TN
LVHW022000060526
838201LV00048B/1632